SUPERNATURAL SUPERHEROES

Heather Trim

www.heatheraine.com

Published by TrimVentures Publishing
www.trimventures.com

ISBN-13: 978-0-9987415-1-2
ISBN-10: 0-9987415-1-5

Cover Art: Vecteezy.com & Heather Trim
Content Illustrations: Heather Trim, Daisy Trim, Daphne Trim, Gabriel Trim, & freeclipart.com

Second Edition

To Daisy, Daphne, Gabriel, Amaryllis, and Violet.
You are my delight and worth the fight.

TABLE OF CONTENTS

WHO, WHAT, WHERE IS GOD?

God is so amazing, it is difficult for humans to describe Him. The Bible is like a code with many mysteries about God and His nature. Here are a few, as stated in the New Testament, about who He is.

1 GOD IS A SPIRIT

"God is spirit, and his worshipers must worship in the Spirit and in truth." John 4:24

A spirit is a person without a body. You can't touch it, you can't see it, but it is real. God is a Spirit. He was never born or created. He has always been alive.

"I am the Alpha and the Omega," says the Lord God, *"who is, and who was, and who is to come, the Almighty."* Revelation 1:8

2 GOD IS LIGHT

This is the message we have heard from him and proclaim to you, that God is light, and in him is no darkness at all. 1 John 1:5

There is no darkness in God because there is no sin in Him. He is the King of Heaven (aka: the Kingdom of Light.) God is good all the time!

Every good and perfect gift is from above, coming down from the Father of the heavenly lights, who does not change like shifting shadows. James 1:17

3 GOD IS A CONSUMING FIRE

"...for our "God is a consuming fire."
Hebrews 12:29

God is called a consuming fire: a fire that utterly consumes or destroys and He will DEVOUR our enemies.

His consuming fire is like the Law of Gravity. Gravity is permanent and powerful on this planet. You can throw things, you can use an engine to fly through the air, but eventually, everything comes down.

4 GOD IS LOVE

"Dear friends,
let us love one another,
for love comes from God.
Everyone who loves
has been born of God
and knows God.
Whoever does not love
does not know God,
because God is love."
1 John 4:7-8

God not only invented love, He IS Love. If God is love, then what exactly is love? 1 Corinthians 13 is the "love chapter" of the Bible and really defines God awesomely.

If Love is... Then God is...

God is patient.
God is kind.
God does not envy.
God does not boast.
God is not proud.
God does not dishonor others.
God is not self-seeking.
God is not easily angered.
God keeps no record of wrongs.
God does not delight in evil.
God rejoices with the truth.
God always protects.
God always trusts.
God always hopes,
God always perseveres.
God never fails.

THE ATTRIBUTES OF GOD

Next up, the attributes of God. (Attributes are characteristics, or details about what someone is like.) There are MANY more attributes of God than this. Here are a few to get you started.

1 GOD IS OMNISCIENT

omni = all
scient = knowing

God has endless knowledge. He knows everything at all times. He knows how many hairs you have on your head. He knows every thought you have. He knows everything about everyone that ever lived and will ever live in the future. He's pretty awesome.

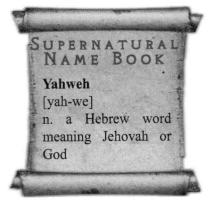

SUPERNATURAL NAME BOOK

Yahweh
[yah-we]
n. a Hebrew word meaning Jehovah or God

2 GOD IS OMNIPOTENT

Omni = all
Potent = powerful

God has very great and unlimited power and authority. He is the most powerful EVER. What kind of power does he have? He can do anything. He can make an entire planet out of nothing. He can breathe into dirt and make a human. He can have a conversation with every person (over 7 billion) on the earth at the same time. That's pretty amazing!

With all that power, He still gives us a choice to love Him or not. He will never make us do something against our will. He will always give us the choice.

Behold, I stand at the door and knock.
If anyone hears my voice and opens the door,
I will come in to him and eat with him, and he with me.
Revelation 3:20

3 GOD IS OMNIPRESENT

omni = all
present = everywhere

Omnipresent means "everywhere at the same time." God is on the earth, in space, and right next to you at the same time. So if He is everywhere, He can see and hear everything all the time because He's not only in every PLACE, but in all TIME: Past, Present, and Future.

God can be described like the wind. The wind is invisible, but you know it is there by the affect it has on everything around it. The wind moves the trees and your hair. God is in every place and time in existence!

Doctor Who can only be in one space and time.

4 GOD NEVER CHANGES

"I the Lord do not change."
Malachi 3:6

God doesn't change. EVER. He is the same Spirit who created the earth as He is today. Some think because the Old and New Testaments show Him very differently that He changed. But the only thing that changed, was us. WE CHANGED. Jesus came, and reconnected us to Him which changes how we relate to Him.

"Jesus Christ is the same yesterday and today and forever."
Hebrews 13:8

5 GOD IS THREE IN ONE

God reveals Himself to His people all throughout the Bible. He tells them, there is only one God. He also presents Himself in three different ways: Father, Son, and Holy Spirit.

All authority in heaven and on earth has been given to me.
Therefore go and make disciples of all nations, baptizing them in
the name of the Father and of the Son and of the Holy Spirit.
Matthew 28:19

WAIT! WHERE IS GOD?

In the spirit realm...

Realm is a word that describes a "place." We live in the physical realm and God resides in the spirit realm. This is a place that we can't always see.

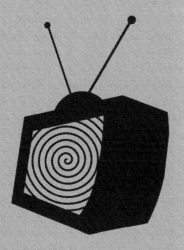

Think about how a television or radio works. The TV station sends out a signal of your favorite show. You can't see the signal, it is invisible, it is sent as radio waves that our eyes can't see. We need a receiver in order to see it. Your television receives that signal and shows you the information in the radio wave.

God lives in a radio-wave-sort-of-place called the Spirit Realm. Angels and demons exist in that place too. The Spirit Realm is called by different names. Heaven, the heavenlies, hell, are all in the spirit realm.

It's possible Adam and Eve could actually SEE God with their human eyes and walk right next to Him. When they sinned, they broke their receivers and lost the special connection with God.

Jesus came and reconnected us to God by sacrificing Himself for us. (Thanks, Jesus, You're the best!) Now we can hear God again. We can speak directly to Him and hear Him talk back!

6 GOD IS ABOUT RELATIONSHIP

God is all about relationship. He created humans to have a friendship with them. He walked with Adam and Eve and talked with them personally. After their sin He never stopped trying to continue a relationship with humans. Even though they broke the connection to Him.

God's Son died to reestablish that personal-supernatural connection. We are so privileged! We get to have a relationship with the Holy Spirit, Jesus, AND the Father, making a connection with all sides of Him.

HIS GREATEST COMMANDMENT

Someone once asked Jesus, "What is the greatest commandment?" (From Moses's Ten Commandments.) Jesus then reveals something about the very nature and heart of God and even what Relationship is.

> *"'Love the Lord your God with all your heart and with all your soul and with all your mind and with all your strength.'*
> *The second is this: 'Love your neighbor as yourself.'*
> *There is no commandment greater than these."*

Mark 12:30-31

LOVE GOD, LOVE PEOPLE AND LOVE YOURSELF!

WHO, WHAT, WHERE IS GOD?

1.   What are 3 things you already knew about God?

2.   What are 3 things you didn't know about God?

3.   What is your FAVORITE thing about God?

Chapter 2

INTRODUCING ANGELS

WHAT ARE ANGELS?

Angels are spirits created by God. Because they are a spirit they do not have a physical body. They live in the spirit realm but they can appear in the physical realm.

Do not forget to show hospitality to strangers, for by so doing some people have shown hospitality to angels without knowing it.
Hebrews 13:2

Even though Angels are spirits (like God) they are not like God in many ways. It is good to know what they can and cannot do. They are not everywhere all the time, they do not know everything, and they are not all-powerful. They cannot hear our thoughts or know what we will do next. Only God does.

WHY?

God created angels to worship Him, to assist Him in taking care of heaven and earth, and to serve mankind, God's favorite creation.

15

THE NATURE OF ANGELS

1 WORSHIPERS

Angels were created to worship God. There is a whole host (group) of angels in heaven just saying, "Holy, holy, holy" about God over and over, worshiping Him endlessly.

Check out what the prophet Isaiah saw:

SUPERNATURAL NAME BOOK

Seraphim
[ser-uh-fim]
n.   celestial   beings hovering above God's throne; the highest order of angels.
Isaiah 6

I saw the Lord, high and exalted, seated on a throne; and the train of his robe filled the temple. Above him were seraphim, each with six wings: With two wings they covered their faces, with two they covered their feet, and with two they were flying. And they were calling to one another:
"Holy, holy, holy is the Lord Almighty;
the whole earth is full of his glory."
At the sound of their voices the doorposts and thresholds shook and the temple was filled with smoke.
Isaiah 6:1b-4

2 GUIDES

Angels have been known to show up and guide people places, like when an angel appeared to the shepherds and told them about Jesus' birth:
"And there were shepherds living out in the fields nearby,
keeping watch over their flocks at night.
An angel of the Lord appeared to them,
and the glory of the Lord shone around them,
and they were terrified. But the angel said to them,
'Do not be afraid. I bring you good news
that will cause great joy for all the people.'"
Luke 2:8-10

3 GUARDIANS

"For he will command his angels
*concerning you to **guard** you*
in all your ways;
they will lift you up in their hands,
so that you will not strike your
foot against a stone."
Psalm 91:11

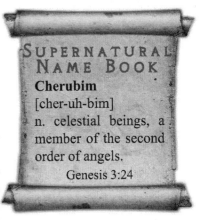

SUPERNATURAL
NAME BOOK
Cherubim
[cher-uh-bim]
n. celestial beings, a
member of the second
order of angels.
Genesis 3:24

God tells angels to guard and protect each of His children. They guard us and help keep us safe. Angels only obey God's commands and because we are in God's family, we are allowed to ask for angelic protection.

The angel of the Lord encamps around those who fear him.
Psalm 34:7

THE SCOOP ON CHERUBIM...

God appointed cherubim to guard the entrance to the Garden of Eden to make sure humans could not find the tree of life.

After he drove the man out,
he placed on the east side of the
Garden of Eden cherubim
and a flaming sword flashing
back and forth
to guard the way to the tree of life.
Genesis 3:24

In the Old Testament, they designed the Ark of the Covenant (a container for the Ten Commandments that was kept in the Tabernacle) with two Cherubim on the top. (Exodus 25)

4 MESSENGERS

GOOD TO KNOW
The Bible was originally written in two languages: Greek and Hebrew.

Angels are God's messengers. The word "angel" translated from the Greek word *angelos* and the Hebrew *malawk*, both mean "messenger."

As a general rule Angels do not sit around and have conversations people when they are delivering a message from God.

God sent the angel Gabriel to Nazareth, a town in Galilee, to a virgin pledged to be married to a man named Joseph, a descendant of David. The virgin's name was Mary. The angel went to her and said, "Greetings, you who are highly favored! The Lord is with you."
Luke 1: 26b-28

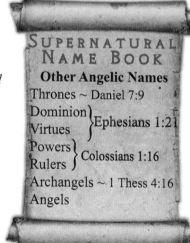

SUPERNATURAL NAME BOOK
Other Angelic Names
Thrones ~ Daniel 7:9
Dominion ⎫
Virtues ⎬ Ephesians 1:21
Powers ⎫
Rulers ⎬ Colossians 1:16
Archangels ~ 1 Thess 4:16
Angels

 SEEING ANGELS

Often, people are scared when they see angels because they are so large and powerful looking. Angels even startled people in Bible times. So angel, Gabriel, begins a message by saying, "Do not be afraid." But don't worry, these amazing spirits are on our side!

The angel said to the women, "Do not be afraid, for I know that you are looking for Jesus, who was crucified."
Matthew 28:5

Think About It

INTRODUCING ANGELS

1. Why did God create angels?

2. Which angelic being has the most contact with humans?

3. Have you ever seen an angel? Describe that experience.

Chapter 3

INTRODUCING EVIL

One day the archangel, Lucifer who stood beside the throne of God decided that he wanted to make himself **"like the Most High."** (Isaiah 14:14.) When angels sin, there is no forgiveness for them. So Lucifer was cast out of heaven and was restricted to darkness.

FALLEN ANGELS = DEMONS

When Satan's sin got him kicked out of heaven, one third of the angels, chose to go with him. (Revelation 12:4) They followed Satan into sin and darkness. Wow, they made a bad choice!

SUPERNATURAL NAME BOOK

archangel
[ahrk-eyn-juh l]
n. a chief or principle angel

*"And the angels who did not keep their positions of authority but abandoned their proper dwelling—these he has kept in **darkness**, bound with everlasting chains for judgment on the great Day."*
Jude 1:6

These "fallen angels" are called demons. This is from the Greek word *daimon* meaning an "evil spirit being lower than God and higher than man."

☆ FYI ☆

There is no such thing as ghosts. Dead people can't roam the earth. Demons cannot create anything, cannot MAKE people do things, and cannot read our minds. Demons can only manipulate people, pretend to be ghosts, pretend to be gods, and cause weird things to happen in order to SEEM like they have more power than they really do.

THE NATURE OF SATAN

1 AGAINST GOD

The name "Satan" is from the Greek word meaning "adversary" or "one who resists." So everything that God IS... Satan is NOT.

God is Love   SATAN IS HATE

God is Love	SATAN IS HATE
God is patient.	Satan is impatient.
God is kind.	Satan is unkind.
God does not envy.	Satan envies.
God does not boast.	Satan boasts.
God is not proud.	Satan is proud.
God does not dishonor others.	Satan dishonors others.
God is not self-seeking.	Satan is very self-seeking.
God is not easily angered.	Satan is very easily angered.
God keeps no record of wrongs.	Satan keeps a record of wrongs.
God does not delight in evil.	Satan delights in evil.
God rejoices with the truth.	Satan resists the truth.
God always protects.	Satan never protects.
God always trusts.	Satan never trusts.
God always hopes,	Satan never hopes,
God always perseveres.	Satan always quits.
God never fails.	Satan always fails.

2 AGAINST HUMANS

Satan and his evil helpers' primary motive is to "steal, kill and destroy." They are determined to destroy those whom the Father loves. God made us to be like Him and He loves us dearly.

The thief comes only to steal, kill and destroy. John 10:10

 STEAL

Steal our attention from God and steal our blessings from Him too!

KILL

Kill our relationship with God. Kill the love between family members and friends. Kill the way we feel about ourselves.

DESTROY

Destroy any chance for love, joy, peace, and all the good things that come from our Father of Heavenly Lights.

3 AN ACCUSER

The word "Devil" is from the Greek word "Diabolos" meaning an "accuser" and a "slanderer." Satan (the devil) is an "accuser of our brothers." (Revelation 12:10b)

Satan spends a lot of time in the heavenlies standing before God's throne accusing us and talking bad about us to God. Which is a big, fat waste of time, because God already knows the truth about us!

That also makes Satan a LIAR!

4 AN UPSIDE DOWN COPYCAT

Since the day Satan decided to sin and tried to make himself higher than God, he turns everything upside down and uses it for EVIL. He counterfeits the work of God in order to deceive us into thinking he is powerful.

But Satan is NOT like God!

★ SATAN IS NOT LIKE GOD ★

Satan is not like God at all. Satan is not everywhere all the time, he is not all-powerful, or all-knowing. He is just a fallen angel who is trying to fight a war against God, that God has already won.

5 SATAN IS NOT OMNIPRESENT

omni = all
present = everywhere

Satan can only be in ONE place at one time. Sometimes Christians yell at him, "Get behind me Satan!" They are wasting energy yelling at someone who isn't even in the room. He is standing before God accusing us.

Many people wrongly believe Satan is omnipresent like the Most High! And that is exactly what he wants us to think!

6 SATAN IS NOT OMNISCIENT

omni = all
scient = knowing

Satan tries to copy how God knows everything by using his band of demons to make it seem like he does.

Satan and his demons have 5,000 years of practice watching people act and react to the lies they tell. They only know our secret sins and pain because they watched what caused it. (Or they caused it.) But they can NOT hear our thoughts.

Demons talk A LOT—like a huge game of "telephone," where they pass information from one to the other to make it seem like they know everything.

7 SATAN IS NOT OMNIPOTENT

Omni = all
Potent = powerful

Demons have no power, no authority, nor do they own anything or anyone. They can't even CREATE anything. All they can do is manipulate and affect people with evil.

Satan is a created being, therefore he cannot have more power than the One who created him. Just like a ROBOT will never be more powerful than the one who built it and can push the "off" button.

Lastly, with all the Power that God has, He doesn't take our choices away, Satan, of course, tries to take all our choices away, to limit us, and lock us away from the freedom God has given us.

IS EVIL STRONGER THAN GOOD?

In nearly every movie ever made, the evil villain is always portrayed as more powerful than the hero. It just might be a conspiracy to lead us to believe that the Devil is stronger. But to figure out the truth, all you have to do is a little math...

GOOD TO KNOW

There are 2 times more angels than demons.

DO THE MATH

Demons want to seem more powerful than God by pretending like there are more demons, than God's angels. God created A LOT of angels, and only one-third of them chose evil. (Revelation 12:4)

96 Trillion x 1/3 = 32 Trillion

We don't actually know how many God created but let's pick a random number. If God created 96 trillion angels, then 32 trillion of them turned to the dark side. And 64 trillion of them are still doing amazing work for God. That's TWICE as many angels than demons in this awesome creation! Demons try to make it seem like there are more of them than the good guys, but it just isn't true. Go Team Angels!

32 Trillion < 64 Trillion

Then, add GOD to the equation. It really isn't a fair fight. God is more powerful than all the angels and demons put together, times INFINITY!

Numbers are not factual but used as an example.

Think About It

INTRODUCING EVIL

1.   What is the primary motive of demons?

2.   How is Satan similar to God?

3.   How is Satan NOT like God?

Chapter 4

EFFECTS OF EVIL

Demons can affect people. (Remember their motive is to Steal, Kill, and Destroy.) The way demons affect people is called: demonization.

DEMONIZATION VS. POSSESSION

Demonization is just a fancy word for a demon affecting someone. Some wrongly call it demon-possession. The word "possess" means "to own something." Demons cannot own you or anything. They can only sneak around and wreck stuff that isn't theirs.

> **HANDY DANDY DICTIONARY**
>
> **Possess**
> [puh-zes]
> v. to have as belonging to one; have as property; own

GUARDIANS VS. STALKERS

If demons copy God and His angels, then they probably assign a demon to stalk each person born on this earth in the same way God assigns a Guardian Angel. Instead of protecting us, demons wait, like a vulture on a branch waiting for a chance to steal, kill and destroy.

WHAT ARE THEY WAITING FOR?

Demons are waiting for a WOUND to form in our spirit. Wounds are formed by WORDS. Curses, mean words, and even words taken the wrong way. Spiritual and moral darkness can then attach to that wound.

Demons have been banished to darkness. If they can find darkness in any human's heart, that is their ticket in.

WHAT IS SPIRITUAL DARKNESS?

We've all heard of sin. Sin is actually anything that hurts a relationship. Stealing candy=sin. Lying to a friend=sin. Hating your brother=sin. Disobeying God=sin. Judging others=sin.

BREAKING RELATIONSHIP = SPIRITUAL DARKNESS = SIN

Hurting someone is sin, whether you do it on purpose or not. Sin creates darkness in our hearts and the enemy is waiting for the chance to attach to that darkness and make it bigger.

WHERE DOES SIN COME FROM?

1. We are born with original sin. (Adam & Eve's big sin, remember?)

2. We are affected by the sins of our parents, grandparents, etc— for generations through the generational curse line. (Ouch!)

3. And... we sin too.

DEMONS ARE SQUATTERS

Our soul is like a house, demons find any way to come inside and make a mess. Kind of like when a house sits dark and empty for a while, people sometimes break in and vandalize them.

If there is darkness (sin) in our hearts, that gives demons an open door. If God is not living in our heart, then there is no way to make the demons LEAVE.

THERE IS HOPE

Jesus came to show us a new way of living in the Kingdom of Light and He showed us the way: Deliverance.

WHO CAN BE DEMONIZED?

Short Answer: ANYONE can be demonized. (Notice I didn't say everyone is.)

Long Answer: Anyone with darkness in their hearts can become demonized. Sadly, by the time kids leave elementary school there is enough build up of darkness, that demons can infest. (It is different for every person.)

"But how can I be demonized? I'm a good Christian person and I'm pretty too," asks the attractive Christian.

RESTRICTED AREA

CHRISTIANS ONLY
BEYOND THIS POINT

DELIVERANCE IS FOR CHRISTIANS ONLY

Jesus did three things: 1. Preached the Good News, 2. Healed the sick, and 3. Cast out demons. He said the very first thing that would mark believers from that time forward was the ministry of deliverance:

And these signs will accompany those who believe:
In my name they will drive out demons;
they will speak in new tongues;
they will pick up snakes with their hands;
and when they drink deadly poison,
it will not hurt them at all;
they will place their hands on sick people,
and they will get well.
Mark 16:17-18

Jesus

Jesus is the door that leads to the Kingdom of God. We are to leave the old behind (which includes demons) and become a new creation. Deliverance is part of the salvation process.

Therefore, if anyone is in Christ, he is a new creation.
The old has passed away; behold, the new has come.
2 Corinthians 5:17

If we do not get rid of the demons when we choose to follow Christ, then the pain of sin and darkness remains in us. We cannot fully heal and we cannot fully become a new creation.

Think About It

AFFECTS OF EVIL

1.   When you were baby, were you born into the Kingdom of Light or the Kingdom of Darkness?

2.   How do you become part of the Kingdom of Light?

3.   How do demons gain permission to affect people?

Chapter 5

THE ESCAPE PLAN

JESUS IS DELIVERANCE

Jesus walked into the synagogue and was handed a scroll of the prophet Isaiah. He declared who he is by telling us his mission.

The Spirit of the Lord is upon me, because he hath anointed me
to preach the gospel to the poor;
he hath sent me to heal the brokenhearted,
to preach deliverance to the captives,
and recovering of sight to the blind,
to set at liberty them that are bruised,
To preach the acceptable year of the Lord.
Luke 4:18 KJV

Jesus rocked our world by saying: I'm here to deliver you... this is my Mission, this is who I Am. He came to save us through DELIVERANCE. He is our salvation. The word "salvation" from the Hebrew words of the Old Testament, and the Greek words of the New Testament **both** translate as deliverance and delivered.

TRANSLATOR

הַעֹושִׁי	σωτηρία
Hebrew to English	Greek to English
SALVATION	SALVATION
yasha'	soteria
[yaw-shaw']	[so-tay-ree'-ah]
to save, to be saved, be	deliverance, preservation,
delivered	safety

PART 1

...to preach the gospel to the poor

Jesus came to fix the broken connection between us and God.

> *For God so loved the world that he gave*
> *his one and only Son, that whoever believes in him*
> *shall not perish but have eternal life. For God did not send*
> *his Son into the world to condemn the world, but to save*
> *the world through him.*
> John 3:16-17

So who is poor? It can't be about money. Let's take supernatural look at what happens in the spirit realm when we accept Jesus: Imagine a pile of dry bones—your spirit was poor and DEAD. Accepting Jesus brings your spirit to life—now those bones come alive. We were poor and dead in spirit, then we are born spiritually by accepting Jesus into our life.

PART 2

...he hath sent me to heal the brokenhearted

BUT! Jesus didn't stop at just reconnecting us to God because we have been broken by that evil Kingdom of Darkness. We are broken from relationships, broken through trauma, broken by mean words and actions. We need healing in our hearts. Everyone is broken because we were born in this sinful world. (Remember that pile of sin?) Brokenness hinders relationships with other people AND even more devastatingly... brokenness blocks relationship with God the Father.

PART 3

...to preach deliverance to the captives,

People are naturally under the influence of evil (born in darkness, living in darkness.) Even when people accept Jesus, they bring their chains and bondage into the Kingdom of Light, the same way they bring their broken hearts into the Kingdom. It doesn't just magically disappear.

Removing demons is part of the salvation process. Two or more people should look for the infestation of demons and through the Power of Jesus' name, send the demons away. (More on that later.)

PART 4

...and recovering of sight to the blind

People in the dark have no need for sight. It's dark, they wouldn't be able to see anything anyway. But when you come into the Kingdom of Light... Whoa! Jesus came to break the power of spiritual darkness and blindness. Normal spiritual life should include seeing, knowing and perceiving life in the spirit realm. It is amazing to SEE with dreams, visions, prophetic words, words of knowledge, words of wisdom and discerning of spirits through the gifts of the Holy Spirit. Jesus is touching our eyes and commanding them to see.

> *I pray also that the eyes of your heart may be enlightened*
> *in order that you may know the hope to which he has called*
> *you, the riches of his glorious inheritance in the saints, and*
> *his incomparably great power for us who believe.*
> Ephesians 1:18-19

PART 5

...to set at liberty them that are bruised

There are several words used in different translations of the Bible for the word "bruised": crushed, broken, wounded. A wounded spirit is more than just being hurt emotionally. It's WAY down deep in a person—so deep it takes your breath away. The Lord is here to take care of wounded people and heal them. And that's pretty much everyone.

> *The Lord is close to the brokenhearted*
> *and saves those who are crushed in spirit.*
> Psalms 34:18

THE SUM UP

...to preach the acceptable year of the Lord.

"The acceptable year" refers to the Year of Jubilee for the Jews (from Leviticus 25.) It was the Sabbath year when debts would be wiped out and slaves set free. Jesus summed up His whole mission to let us know we are now in a time of Total Acceptance. If we follow Him down these 5 steps into the Kingdom of Light we receive liberty from every sort of bondage, from the debt of sin, from emotional destruction, from spiritual bondage, from spiritual blindness, and from deep woundedness. We are totally accepted by God to have a close relationship with Him if we receive His Son.

THE CENTERPIECE

1. good news to poor/dead
2. healing for brokenness
3. *DELIVERANCE* to captive
4. sight to blind
5. liberty for wounded

We cannot be truly "whole" without Deliverance from demonization.

THE ESCAPE PLAN

1. Why do Christians need deliverance?

2. Whose name do we use to drive out demons?

3. Would you like to get deliverance?

Chapter 6

PROPHETIC DELIVERANCE

So if the Son sets you free, you will be free indeed.
John 8:36

Jesus set us free from death, brokenness, blindness, and wounds. But what if there is something sabotaging the work of the Holy Spirit? If there is an evil spirit still lurking, it is actively wounding us and undoing what Jesus came to do. It's like trying to dig a hole with the enemy standing behind us kicking the dirt back in. So God made Deliverance the centerpiece of salvation but deliverance doesn't AUTOMATICALLY occur when we decide to follow Jesus.

GOD'S GIFTS IN DELIVERANCE

Deliverance is a supernatural event and God has given us many gifts to connect with Him and His spirit realm. We use several in a deliverance session: Prophecy and Discerning between Spirits.

1 PROPHECY

Follow the way of love and eagerly desire spiritual gifts, especially the gift of prophecy.
I Corinthians 14:1

We talk ONLY to God about whether there are demons affecting someone and what they are doing. If we asked the demons, they would lie. God is the only one who will tell us the truth, through the gift of Prophecy. What's great, is that we all have the ability to hear God's Voice.

2 DISTINGUISH BETWEEN SPIRITS

In order to tell a demon to leave, we have to find out their name or job title. (Demons are like lawyers, if we don't do it the "right way" they find a loophole to stay.) So God shares the gift of discerning between spirits to help us figure out what their name or job title is. We most often just find the job title (also known as their "function.") Some of their jobs/functions are: fear, rejection, hinderer, destroyer, control, etc.

DELIVERANCE SESSION DETAILS

If you decide you would like to get deliverance, the session looks similar to a quiet prayer meeting. In your deliverance session you will sit in the middle of the room with the deliverance team members sitting all around (to see all the way around you) because the spirit realm is 3D.

WHY A TEAM FOR DELIVERANCE?

Two or three prophets should speak, and the others should weigh what is said.
I Corinthians 14:29

Deliverance should NOT be done by one person. We are told to test a prophetic word from two or three people. If there is only one person doing deliverance, who will test what they say?

No one can do deliverance on themselves, just as no one can see the middle of their own back. We need someone else to look at our whole self to find what is ailing us.

DELIVERANCE PLAY–BY–PLAY

1 WORSHIP

The Team Leader will start with Worship because this is about God. He is the reason we can have deliverance from our enemies and it sets up an atmosphere of Honor for Him. Your ears, the team's ears, and the demon's ears must hear that what we do is all about FATHER—not us.

PROTECTION 2

We will ask for protection over everyone involved—You, the team, and intercessors. The Leader will pray protection over all aspects of our lives—family, home, school, and stuff. Angels are called in to surround the place where the deliverance is happening.

> *The angel of the Lord encamps around*
> *those who fear him, and he delivers them.*
> Psalm 34:7

3 COMMAND

The Team Leader will command the demons to be silent and not to move or manifest using the source of our authority: Jesus.

"Jesus Christ if Nazareth, the Son of the Living God,
the One who died on the cross, rose again on the third day
and is now interceding for us on the right side of the Father."

We will also admit to our weakness and that we have no authority, power, strength or dominion of our own. But we don't come in our own name. We come in the POWERFUL name of Jesus!

RELEASE THE GIFTS 4

We invite the Holy Spirit to release His awesome gifts needed for deliverance, especially discerning between spirits.

5 SUBMIT OUR MINDS

We then submit our mind and thoughts to the Holy Spirit. We don't use our physical eyes, or natural knowledge, or first impressions about the person receiving deliverance. We give our thoughts to God and exchange them for His thoughts.

We take captive every thought to make it obedient to Christ.
II Corinthians 10:5

But we have the mind of Christ.
I Corinthians 2:16

DISCERN 6

We ask Holy Spirit THREE specific questions:

1. What is the name of the **chief and ruling spirit**? This is the highest ranking spirit on, attached to, or harassing the person. If you cut off the "head" of a snake, the body will die. So if we tell the ruling spirit (the leader) and any other demons under it's command, they will ALL go.

2. Is there a **generational curse line**? This is simply a feeder tube of DARKNESS. The affects of sin is passed down from generation to generation. (Parents to children, to the 10th generation.)

3. Is there a **spirit of false religion**? This type of demon (when it's not the ruling spirit) must be addressed separately.

7 BREAK CURSE LINE

We will use the "Sword of the Spirit" to cut the curse line. The Sword is the Word of God: the Bible. We will read just a couple verses swinging the Power of His Word.

8 CAST OUT DEMONS

Speaking directly to the chief and ruling spirit, the Team Leader will tell it to leave in the Name of Jesus, as well as all other demons under its authority. There will be no shouting and no getting all worked up.

WEIRD SIDENOTE

Some people believe superstitions that say a person needs to sneeze, burp, yawn, or vomit to release demons. These are totally unneccessary. A person just has to be willing to have them go.

We also tell them WHERE to go: "Leave this spiritual territory chased by the Angel of the Lord." That way they are far away from you. We operate in the Gift of Discernment and will know that they are all gone.

TURN ON THE LIGHT 9

We ask the Holy Spirit to come as Light (remember that God is Light!) He floods the spirit realm with His Light and we can see or sense whether the dark spirits are gone.

DELIVERANCE DONE! ✔

HEALING JUMP START

Deliverance is like surgery—removing demons is like removing a tumor from your wounded soul. After surgery, you need to be cleaned up and given medication to start healing.

Deliverance is a supernatural event and healing will also be supernatural. So we use a metaphor for healing taken from the story of the Good Samaritan in Luke 10:30-37. (Which is the same routine paramedics use when they help an injured person.)

"He went to him and bandaged his wounds, pouring on oil and wine. Then he put the man on his own donkey, took him to an inn and took care of him." Luke 10: 34

THE
WOUNDED SPIRIT
PRAYER

THE WINE

The Good Samaritan used wine as an antiseptic to CLEANSE a wound and is also a picture of the *blood of Jesus.*

FIRST, we apply the Cleansing Wine of the Blood of Jesus
- To your mind & memories, what you've seen, heard, and spoken
- To your heart ~ your emotions
- To the Inmost Place ~ your spirit

THE OIL

The Good Samaritan then used oil as a HEALING balm, like using Triple Antibiotic Ointment. The oil of the Holy Spirit brings healing.

SECOND, we apply the Healing Oil of the Holy Spirit
- To your mind & memories, what you've seen, heard, and spoken
- To your heart ~ your emotions
- To the Inmost Place ~ your spirit

BANDAGE THE WOUNDS

THIRD, we wrap you in the presence of God the Father
The Good Samaritan brought the wounded man "to the inn." This inn, is a picture of God's Presence. We wrap you in the Presence of God for protection as you heal.

FILL THE HOUSE WITH LIGHT

Now that the demons are no longer "squatting" in your house. We ask for a fresh infilling of the Holy Spirit. Someone will live in the House of Your Soul, whether Dark or Light. So when demons peek at your soul, we want the Holy Spirit to answer the door in His robe and bunny slippers, showing that this is HIS home now.

> *When an evil spirit comes out of a man, it goes through arid places seeking rest and does not find it. Then it says, "I will return to the house I left." When it arrives, it finds the house unoccupied, swept clean and put in order. Then it goes and takes with it seven other spirits more wicked than itself, and they go in and live there. And the final condition of that man is worse than the first.*
> Matthew 12:43-45

FYI

It might take you longer to read this whole chapter than it will to go through a deliverance session. Generally, it will all happen in the matter of 15 to 20 minutes. And because everything is happening in the spirit realm where our physical eyes can't see, it will seem really boring, like nothing is happening, in a quiet prayer meeting.

So try not to fall asleep.

PROPHETIC DELIVERANCE

1. What supernatural gifts are generally used in deliverance?

2. Why do we have to find the "Chief and Ruling Spirit" in a deliverance session?

3. Why don't we ask the demons what their name or function is?

Chapter 7

SUPERNATURAL HEALING PLAN

What do I do now?

As a young person going through deliverance, you don't have years and years of pain and muck to get over. Most people get deliverance when they are old and wrinkly. You now have an opportunity to heal SOONER and go FARTHER in the Kingdom of Light. The big question that everyone asks, old and young, is How do I heal? Here are two simple things to get you started: **Find God** and **Change the way you think**.

FIND GOD

If God is all about relationship, then it's time to get to know Him. Go find Him. He loves to play hide and seek. He hides in the best hiding spots. The first place you could look is in the Bible. Talk to people that love Him.

How do you get to know a human? Do you talk to them? Ask them questions? Same with God. He talks differently than anyone you know.

(See the list of resources in the back of this book for ideas of where to hunt God down.)

TRANSFORM

Since the enemy was sabotaging us from the inside, it was REALLY hard to change the way we think from Kingdom of Darkness thinking into Kingdom of Light thinking. Now that the enemy is gone, it's time to transform the way you think.

Do not conform to the pattern of this world, but be transformed by the renewing of your mind. Then you will be able to test and approve what God's will is—his good, pleasing and perfect will.

Romans 12:2

It's time to find your wounds and heal them. Find those lies you believe about yourself and trade them for the Truth. Here is a simple healing step-by-step to use when you find a wound.

THE FIVE WHOLENESS STEPS

Identify the wound

Confess the core belief

Hand it to Jesus

Invite the Holy Spirit

Make Kingdom declarations

1 Identify the Wound

All humans are trying to figure out who they are. Am I loved? Am I valued? Most often we believe the lies this broken world tells us rather than God's truth about how valuable and lovable we are.

"As a man thinks in his heart, so is he." Proverbs 23:7

As painful emotions (like anger or fear) and problem behaviors (like bad attitudes or disobeying) come up, find out WHY you feel or act that way. Have a conversation with yourself:

"Why am I so mad right now?"
　　　"Because my brother called me stupid."
"Is that true?"
　　　"No."
"But you wouldn't be mad if someone told you that you were a seven-foot purple noodle."
　　　"No, I would just laugh."
"Then you must believe that you're stupid if it bothered you that much."
　　　"Oh, snap!"

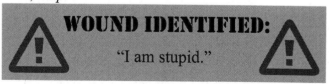

WOUND IDENTIFIED:

"I am stupid."

2 Confess the Core Belief

Tell your Heavenly Father what you just found. Share how it has affected how you feel and how you behave.

> *"If we confess our sins* **(our lies, Kingdom of Darkness thinking)**,
> *he is faithful and just to forgive us our sins,*
> *and to cleanse us from all unrighteousness."*
> I John 1:9 (Parenthesis mine)

WOUND CONFESSED:

"Father, I believed that I am stupid. I get mad and want to say mean things to people who hurt my feelings."

3 Hand it to Jesus

Take that "darkness thinking" and arrest it just like a policeman and take it downtown to Jesus' Police Station. Hand it over for Jesus to deal with.

WOUND HANDED OVER:

"Jesus, I give you this belief that I am stupid."

> *"Bring into captivity every thought to the obedience of Christ."*
> II Corinthians 10:5b

4 Invite God's Presence

You don't have to send Him a fancy invitation, all you have to say is,

"Holy Spirit come and heal me."

Ask the Holy Spirit to connect you to the Presence of God, the supernatural healing ointment to heal your wounds.

5 Make Kingdom Declarations

After removing the Darkness thinking, we can then add the Kingdom of Light thinking. Ask God for a revelation of His Truth in 2 ways:

Ask Him to speak to you with love and positive affirmation. Learn to hear God. You will know it's Him because He will always say something that lines up with the Bible.

⚠ KINGDOM DECLARATION ALERT! ⚠

"God created humans in His Image,
and He said we are very good!"

Speak His Truth from the Word of God over yourself. Speak it out loud. There is power in the spoken word. Put it out there to overwrite that lie.

Find a Bible verse and speak it **out loud** into your wound.

For, "Who has known the mind of the Lord
so as to instruct him?" But we have the mind of Christ.
1 Corinthians 2:16

AM I HEALED YET?

If you go to the doctor and he gives you a prescription for medicine to heal an infected cut on your leg, he would tell you to continue to use it until you are healed. So how often should you use the Five Wholeness Steps?
Any time you are hurt, anytime you find a lie. Keep using it until it doesn't hurt anymore. How do you know if it doesn't hurt anymore?
Well, the next time someone calls you stupid, you'll know!

I.C.HIM

SUPERNATURAL HEALING PLAN

1. When should you use the Five Wholeness Steps?

2. What wounds have you found?

3. What what is God's Truth about you?

Chapter 8

SUPERNATURAL SUPERHEROES

God is all about relationship, which is why He sent Jesus to reconnect us to Him. Remember the three relationships God encourages? Being supernatural superheroes is as simple as "Love God, Love Yourself, and Love Each Other."

1 LOVE GOD – THE POWER SOURCE

Now it's time to start exploring your connection to God and learning to hear God for yourself. He can hear your thoughts and you can hear His. Get to know what He sounds like.

We all talk to ourselves inside our own heads when we are making a decision or thinking about the day. You know your own inner voice. Take a moment to quiet your busy brain, ask Him a question and anticipate an answer. Stop talking and listen. Practice listening. Find out what He sounds like.

A UNIQUE CONNECTION

What does God sound like? God speaks to us in different ways because we are all so different. God speaks every language on earth: 6,500 languages!

There is no wrong way to hear God. To some, He is a voice in their head. To others, He talks in pictures. To someone else, He speaks through movie quotes. Some hear Him through Bible verses, and some get a wordless idea in their mind.

In whatever way He communicates best with you, get to know Him. He's pretty amazing.

2 LOVE YOURSELF – YOU ARE THE SUPERHERO

As it is written: "For your sake
we face death all day long;
we are considered as sheep
to be slaughtered."
No, in all these things
we are more than conquerors
through him who loved us.
For I am convinced that neither death nor life,
neither angels nor demons,
neither the present nor the future,
nor any powers, neither height nor depth,
nor anything else in all creation,
will be able to separate us from the love of God
that is in Christ Jesus our Lord.
Romans 8:36-39

You are a valuable part of the Kingdom of Light. You are a gift to your family, your community, your school, and your world. You truly don't have to DO anything in order to be loved by God. You are alive, therefore He loves you. You breathe, therefore you are acceptable. You can just BE you because God loves you eternally.

Many superheroes have a learning period where they have to come to accept WHO they are and the power within. We have God's Power within us when we accept Jesus—"we are more than conquerors." You are the superhero. It's time to figure out your true identity and how to live with His Power in you.

FINDING YOUR TRUE IDENTITY

Here are a few ideas to search and discover yourself:

Figure out what kind of **PERSONALITY** you have and be the healthiest version of that personality EVER.

Are you an **INTROVERT** or **EXTROVERT**? Do you gain energy by being alone or with people?

What is your **LOVE LANGUAGE**? How do you feel loved? How do you show love to others?

What's your **BIRTH ORDER**? First children behave differently than last children and middle children--which are you?

(See the RESOURCES section for websites and books about finding your identity.)

WITH GREAT POWER COMES GREAT RESPONSIBILITY

Why is it important to know yourself?

Knowing yourself is first ACCEPTING who you are so that you can LOVE yourself. There is power in knowing your strengths and limitations. Spiderman had to figure out how to shoot his webs and swing from them. Superman had to figure out how he was limited by kryptonite. You are responsible for finding out who you are and choose to love whoever you find.

Have you ever met someone who acts totally fake? Or always hateful? A lot of times, that means they don't love themselves.

Everyone wants to meet REAL friends and share who they really are. Who you are is a gift to the people around you. And the way you love yourself, is the way you'll love your family, friends, enemies, and God. So its important to love yourself.

3 LOVE EACH OTHER –

What is love REALLY? God gave us a pretty hefty description in the Bible. Patience, kindness, not envying (which is wanting what someone has), not selfish, etc. (See page 8 for the full list.)

If we are impatient with our brother, we are hating on him. If we are unkind to our mom, we are being hateful to her. If we want what our best friend has (an iPad, a bike, a car, access to WiFi, etc) we are actually HATING our best friend.

So it's time we build relationships on True Love. Sharing who we are with family or friends with patience, kindness, and more. Then we can share our supernatural superpowers with love. Then there are no mixed messages between love and hate coming out of us.

SHARING SUPERNATURAL GIFTS

"In the last days, God says,
I will pour out my Spirit on all people.
Your sons and daughters will prophesy,
your young men will see visions,
your old men will dream dreams.
Even on my servants, both men and women,
I will pour out my Spirit in those days,
and they will prophesy.
I will show wonders in the heavens above
and signs on the earth below,
blood and fire and billows of smoke.
The sun will be turned to darkness
and the moon to blood
before the coming of the great
and glorious day of the Lord.
And everyone who calls
on the name of the Lord will be saved."
Acts 2:17-21

We live in the best time in history! Before Jesus came, God had to specifically go to each of His prophets and anoint them to speak His Words. But Jesus came, reconnected us to the Holy Spirit, and gave many gifts for EVERY person on this earth.

As you begin to hear God, share what He is telling you with other people. Some people naturally function in one (or two) supernatural gifts but we have access to all of God's Gifts. They are the cool gadgets in our superhero tool belt meant to help and ENCOURAGE each other.

ASK FOR SUPER POWERS

You might already have an idea that you are special—maybe you can see in the spirit realm. Or you may have no idea what is possible with the Holy Spirit. Either way, it's time to use your "receivers" that have been reconnected to God and use the gifts He has given.

If you know His Voice, you can access any of the gifts in the Bible. The Gifts of the Holy Spirit are ALL available to ALL of us ALL the time. He is our Dad, after all! And all we have to do is ask...

> *For everyone who asks receives;*
> *the one who seeks finds;*
> *and to the one who knocks,*
> *the door will be opened.*
> Matthew 7:8

Ask Him for a vision. Ask Him for a dream. Ask Him for the interpretation. Practice hearing God in your awake hours and your sleeping hours. Ask, ask ask! Our Father loves to give gifts!

WORD OF KNOWLEDGE Healing
Visions Prophecy Miracles
Faith Dreams Word of Wisdom
SPEAK IN TONGUES
interpretation of tongues
Distinguishing Between Spirits

1 Corinthians 12:7-10

Think About It

SUPERNATURAL SUPERHEROES

1. What is the unique way you hear God?

2. How do you show love to others?

3. Which Supernatural Gifts come natural to you?

RESOURCES

LEARNING ABOUT GOD

- **The Holy Bible**

- **A Shepherd Looks at Psalm 23** by Phillip Keller

LEARNING ABOUT YOURSELF

- **Color Code Personality Profile**: Go to www.colorcode.com to take their free online personality test. Read more about each personality color on their blog or the book: **The People Code** by Dr. Taylor Hartman

- **The Five Love Languages**: Go to www.5lovelanguages.com and take their free online love language test. You can also read their teen version of their book: **The 5 Love Languages of Teenagers** by Gary Chapman

- **The Birth Order Book** by Dr. Kevin Leman

- **Wild At Heart** by John Eldredge (For guys)

- **Captivating** by John & Stasi Eldredge (For girls)

HEALING YOURSELF

- **The Five Wholeness Steps** by Katie Mather

- **Search for Significance** (Student Edition) by Robert S. McGee

- **How to Stop the Pain** by Dr. James B. Richards

ABOUT THE AUTHOR

Heather Trim is an award-winning author, conference speaker and cookie eater. With over 23 years in ministry, she works alongside her parents, Tim and Katie Mather, at Bear Creek Ranch, a Christian retreat center.

In addition to SUPERNATURAL SUPERHEROES, Heather is the author of WINGBOUND, a young adult fantasy novel, with several more fiction books in the works.

Creativity brings her life. If she isn't writing, graphic designing, bullet journaling, or reading, she's probably out gazing at the clouds daydreaming and wishing she had wings.

FOLLOW HER ONLINE:

Website: www.heatheraine.com
Email: heather@heatheraine.com
Facebook: facebook.com/heatherainetrim
Instagram: instagram.com/heatheraine5
Twitter: twitter.com/heatheraine

Bear Creek Ranch: www.BCRcamp.com

Made in the USA
Columbia, SC
18 April 2019